This book belongs to:

_____

This book is dedicated to cat lovers everywhere.

Published 2023 by Flowered Press
Copyright©2023 by Hayley Rose

Text and design by Hayley Rose
Illustrations by Bright Jungle Studios

ISBN: 978-1-950842-34-6

Library of Congress Control Number: 2022913650

All rights reserved.
No part of this publication may be reproduced, stored in a retrieval system or transmitted by any form or by any means, electronic, recording or otherwise without the prior permission in writing from the publisher.

Flowered Press
8776 E.Shea Blvd., #106-213
Scottsdale, AZ 85260

www.HayleyRose.com

Stella the Stinky Cat
A Fart-Filled Tale

Written by Hayley Rose

Illustrated by Bright Jungle Studios

Stella the cat has a problem.
She toots A LOT!

PEE-EW

AND... she toots
when walking across the piano.

Stella the cat has a problem.
She toots A LOT!

PEE-EW

She toots on the piano.
AND... she toots during Caturday celebrations.

Stella the cat has a problem.
She toots A LOT!

She toots on the piano.
She toots at Caturday celebrations.
She toots enjoying a beverage from the toilet.
AND... she toots when playing with her favorite cat toys.

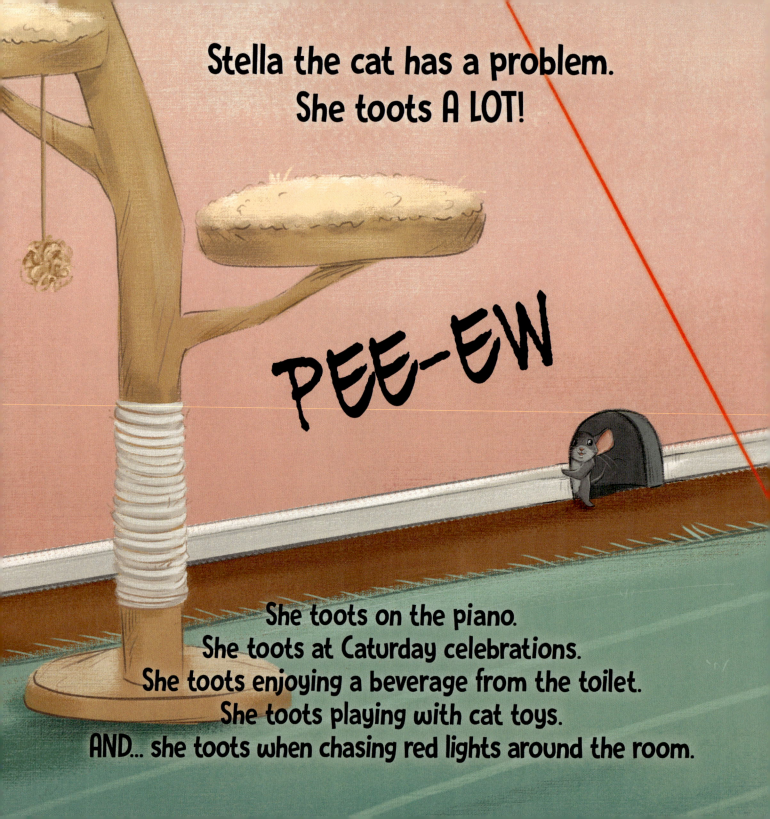

Stella the cat has a problem.
She toots A LOT!

PEE-EW

She toots on the piano.
She toots at Caturday celebrations.
She toots enjoying a beverage from the toilet.
She toots playing with cat toys.
AND... she toots when chasing red lights around the room.

She's a CRAZY, smarty, drinky, party, plinky, stinky cat.

She's a FLIRTY, crazy, smarty, drinky, party, plinky, stinky cat.

Stella the cat has a problem.
She toots A LOT!

PEE-EW

She toots on the piano.
She toots at Caturday celebrations.
She toots enjoying a beverage from the toilet.
She toots playing with cat toys.
She toots chasing after red lights.
She toots meeting new cats.
AND... she toots when taking a bath.

Stella the cat has a problem.
She toots A LOT!

PEE-EW

She toots on the piano.
She toots at Caturday celebrations.
She toots enjoying a beverage from the toilet.
She toots playing with cat toys.
She toots chasing after red lights.
She toots meeting new cats.
She toots taking a bath.
AND... she toots when rummaging through garbage cans for treats.

Stella the cat has a problem.
She toots A LOT!

PEE-EW

She toots on the piano.
She toots at Caturday celebrations.
She toots enjoying a beverage from the toilet.
She toots playing with cat toys.
She toots chasing after red lights.
She toots meeting new cats.
She toots taking a bath.
She toots rummaging through garbage cans for treats.
AND... she toots when lounging in her cat tree.

Stella the cat has a problem.
She toots A LOT!

PEE-EW

She toots on the piano.
She toots at Caturday celebrations.
She toots enjoying a beverage from the toilet.
She toots playing with cat toys.
She toots chasing after red lights.
She toots meeting new cats.
She toots taking a bath.
She toots rummaging through garbage cans for treats.
She toots lounging in her cat tree.
AND... she toots when pouncing through the air.

Stella the cat has a problem.
She toots A LOT!

PEE-EW

She toots on the piano.
She toots at Caturday celebrations.
She toots enjoying a beverage from the toilet.
She toots playing with cat toys.
She toots chasing after red lights.
She toots meeting new cats.
She toots taking a bath.
She toots rummaging through garbage cans for treats.
She toots lounging in her cat tree.
She toots pouncing through the air.
AND... she toots when resting in the summer sun.

Here are a few fun cat facts:

Cats can jump up to 6 times their height.

The oldest cat in the world was 38 years old.

In 1963, a cat went to space.

Cats sleep for around 13 to 16 hours a day.

A group of cats is called a clowder or a glaring.

Cats can run up to 30 mph.

A cat was the mayor of an Alaskan town for 20 years.

Cats dream.

Made in the USA
Las Vegas, NV
04 December 2022